DIGITAL RETIREMENT

REPLACE YOUR SOCIAL SECURITY INCOME IN THE NEXT 12 MONTHS & RETIRE EARLY

Wealth With Words

MICHELLE KULP

Copyright © 2020 Michelle Kulp

Published by: Monarch Crown Publishing

ISBN: 978-1-7354188-2-7

All rights reserved. No part of this book may be reproduced or transmitted in any form or by any means, electronic or mechanical, including photocopying, recording, or by any information storage and retrieval system, without written permission of the author, except for the inclusion of brief quotations in a review.

Disclaimer

This publication is designed to provide accurate and authoritative information with regard to the subject matter covered. It is sold with the understanding that the publisher is not engaged in rendering legal, accounting, or other professional advice. If legal advice or other expert assistance is required, the services of a competent professional should be sought.

The author wishes to acknowledge the respective sources for use of graphs, charts, and other data in this book, and it is the author's intent to portray that data accurately rather than through representations.

This book may contain technical or other errors. Michelle Kulp, Monarch Crown Publishing and Spirit Wealth, LLC do not guarantee its accuracy, completeness, or suitability. In no event shall Michelle Kulp, Monarch Crown Publishing and Spirit Wealth, LLC be liable for any special, indirect, or consequential damages relating to this material for any use of this material or for any referenced website and courses, or the application of any idea or strategy in this book.

The information contained in this book is provided by Michelle Kulp, Monarch Crown Publishing and Spirit Wealth, LLC, and it is offered for educational and informational purposes only. Michelle Kulp is a not a licensed financial planner. She suggests that you consult with a qualified legal or tax-planning professional with regard to your personal circumstances. Nothing in this book should be interpreted or construed as legal, regulatory, insurance, tax, or financial planning advice or as an offer to perform services related to any of these fields in any respect.

The content of this book contains general information and may not reflect current legal, tax, insurance, or regulatory developments and information, and it is not guaranteed to be correct, complete, or current. Michelle Kulp, Monarch Crown Publishing and Spirit Wealth, LLC make no warranty, expressed or implied, as to the accuracy or reliability of this information or the information contained in any referenced website or course.

Readers of this book should not act or refrain from acting on the basis of any information included herein without seeking appropriate legal or other relevant advice related to the particular facts and circumstances at issue from an attorney or other advisor duly and properly licensed in the recipient's state of residence. Michelle Kulp, Monarch Crown Publishing and Spirit Wealth, LLC expressly disclaim all liability with respect to actions taken or not taken by the reader based on any or all of the information or other contents within this book or provided by Michelle Kulp directly. Any information sent to Michelle Kulp, Monarch Crown Publishing and Spirit Wealth, LLC via Internet, e-mail, or through any referenced website is not secure and is done so on a non-confidential basis.

Should the reader of this book seek a referral to any service provider, the person to whom such referral is made is solely responsible for assessing the knowledge, skill, or capabilities of such provider, and neither the author, presenter, nor Michelle Kulp, Monarch Crown Publishing and Spirit Wealth, LLC are responsible for the quality, integrity, performance, or any other aspect of any services ultimately provided by such provider or any damages, consequential or incidental, arising from the use of such provider. Any opinions expressed in the book are mine alone and mine based on the information publicly available to me in my interpretation of that information.

TABLE OF CONTENTS

INTRODUCTION 1
CHAPTER 1: THE RETIREMENT CRISIS 9
CHAPTER 2: GET RICH SLOW IS A LOSING GAME 19
CHAPTER 3: 4 SECRETS TO WEALTH 27
CHAPTER 4: SHORTCUTS TO SUCCESS 39
CHAPTER 5: HOW TO AVOID WRITING CRAPPY BOOKS 47
CHAPTER 6: REVERSE-ENGINEERING YOUR BESTSELLER 71
CHAPTER 7: NOTHING HAPPENS UNTIL YOU LAUNCH 81
CHAPTER 8: THE BOOK-A-MONTH (BAM) FRAMEWORK 93
CHAPTER 9: SOCIAL SECURITY REPLACEMENT BLUEPRINT 107
CHAPTER 10: CLOSING THOUGHTS 117
RESOURCES 121

"I grew up believing that one day my prince would come. He would whisk me off my feet and we'd fly blissfully into the sunset. I spent much of my life searching for this prince. Several times I thought I had found him. Each time I was wrong. But I kept looking. I kept waiting. Then one day, as if jolted awake from a deep sleep, I realized that Prince Charming wasn't coming. The realization hit me with the force of a tidal wave, and I knew my life would never be the same again.

That was the day I shifted my focus from 'out there' and began to take a long, hard look at myself. What I saw was life-changing. I discovered that I had wings. These wings had been with me since the day I was born, but somewhere along the way I learned that a prince wouldn't be attracted to a woman who could fly. Afraid and discouraged, I tucked my wings away, and they shriveled from disuse. Eventually I forgot they'd ever existed. But suddenly, on that day of awakening, I felt their presence again—the little flutters, the tiny surge of power. I knew that with a bit of effort, I could soar like a bird, go wherever I wanted to go, accomplish what I'd never believed was possible.

I have since come to realize something else. I am not alone. Each of us was born with wings. Each of us has the ability to go farther than we ever thought possible, to do things beyond our wildest imaginings. *Prince Charming Isn't Coming* is meant to be about far more than money. It is about waking up, reclaiming our power, remembering we can fly."

Excerpt from *Prince Charming Isn't Coming* by Barbara Stanny

INTRODUCTION

It's time to renounce Prince Charming and start relying on ourselves instead, especially when it comes to our retirement and financial future.

Prince Charming is an outside projection that something or someone, real or imagined, will save you. Here are some *Prince Charming* projections many of us have about our financial future:

- Someone will come and fix all of my financial problems.
- My pension will support me in retirement.
- The government will take care of me with Social Security.
- My 401K will provide for me and my family when I retire.

An article[1] on Nasdaq.com states:

> "A whopping 64% of U.S. workers are expected to retire with less than $10,000 in dedicated retirement savings, according to a new survey by GOBankingRates. And when we dig into how that statistic breaks down, things look even bleaker. That's because 45% of respondents say they have no money set aside for retirement at all. Meanwhile, 19% expect to leave the workforce with less than $10,000, which is basically akin to retiring broke.

---

[1] https://www.nasdaq.com/articles/64-of-americans-are-at-risk-of-retiring-broke-2019-09-30

The other 36% of Americans aren't necessarily in such great shape, either. A good 20% say they think they'll retire with somewhere between $10,000 and $100,000. But even the latter isn't a whole lot of money in the grand scheme of what could easily be a 20-year retirement or more. And while the fact that just over 12% of respondents think they'll retire with anywhere from $100,000 to just under $500,000 is more encouraging, that's a pretty wide gap, and those closer to the lower end of that spectrum are still in pretty big trouble.

All told, only about 4% of Americans expect to retire with $500,000 or more. If you're not one of them, and you've already been working for quite some time, then it means you have some serious catching up to do."

When I read this article, I thought about my own precarious situation…

After contributing to my 401K for 17 long years while working as a paralegal, I thought the income from my 401K account, combined with my future Social Security, would be enough to support me in my golden years.

Then life happened…

In 2007, I purchased a million-dollar home with my then-fiancé right before the housing market crash and within a short time (months), the value of that home dropped by almost 50%. On top of that, my fiancé and I split up and he left me with 100% of the bills on said million-dollar home. Did I mention I was also a single mom raising three children with minimal child support?

MY 401K BECAME THE CASH COW

In an attempt to *save my home*, I started pulling out cash from my 401K, taking penalties and hits regularly to pay the bills and keep the million-dollar house afloat. Additionally, my six figure salary as an outside sales rep. suddenly was reduced to half.

I was unprepared is an understatement.

Three attorneys and five years later, I walked away from the million-dollar house in a short sale and had depleted my 401K savings down to ZERO.

They say "hope springs eternal" because no matter what happens to us in life, we always have hope. Even when it appears as if we've arrived at a dead-end with no other options, a new road miraculously appears.

That new road for me was *self-publishing*.

I was fortunate to have started my online business (www.becomea6figurwoman.com) in 2005 and built a six-figure business with multiple streams of income over the next 15 years. However, none of those income streams were from passive income.

In December of 2019, I read an article by Written Word Media[2] that said the average author making $100K each year had 28 books in their catalog. The thought immediately popped into my head, "I'm going to start writing a book a month and create a SIX-FIGURE PASSIVE INCOME."

---

[2] www.writtenwordmedia.com/author-income-how-to-make-a-living-from-your-writing/

I've always loved to write, and was lucky enough to rediscover my passion after a chance encounter with Billy Ray Cyrus in 1992. You can read the full story about this transformational meeting on my website:

https://www.becomea6figurewoman.com/about/

I began the experiment of writing a book a month in January 2020 to see what would happen and if I could create six figures in passive income from my writing. I'm happy to tell you that just nine months into my *experiment*, I have already created $2,300 in monthly income, which is more than what I'll receive from Social Security *some day* and is also enough to cover my housing expenses in full.

Think about this – I contributed to my 401K for 17 years, and the money was depleted because of one BIG emergency. Now, I have created $2,300+ a month in passive income in just nine short months! In 18 months, I should be earning $4,600+ a month in passive income from royalties. That's enough to cover ALL of my living expenses and retire right now if I wanted to.

If and when I collect Social Security, that will be gravy because my bills are already paid in full.

SIX FIGURES IS IN MY FUTURE

I plan on creating six figures in passive income in the next 12-18 months with the royalties from my writing as well as from my online programs. Obviously, this strategy takes some time, but the time and money invested in this endeavor is 100% worth it! I'm not relying on *Prince Charming* to save me—I can save myself.

Do you know how much you will be paid from Social Security when you retire?

According to www.smartasset.com[3], if you have an annual income of $50,000 (which is a little higher than the median income in the U.S.) and contribute for 35 years, you could begin claiming Social Security at age 62 to the tune of $22,042 per year, which is $1,836 per month.

I've already exceeded that amount in nine months by publishing a book a month on Amazon.

---

[3] https://smartasset.com/

CREATE YOUR OWN INCOME

Recently, one of my clients, Daniel Rondberg, a Retirement Expert, joined my www.bestsellingauthorprogram.com. When Daniel discovered my plan to write a book a month to create passive income, he immediately joined me on this journey. Daniel pointed out that my plan was brilliant and said, "All investment vehicles (real estate, the stock market, etc.) have one purpose and that is to *buy income*." So naively, I was creating my own investment vehicle and retirement income!

Daniel contributed an upcoming chapter in this book, which details the Retirement Crisis and explains how my system gives you a 240% ROI (higher than any other investment vehicle I know of).

In May 2020, I wrote a #1 bestselling book, "28 Books to $100K," which focuses on writing, self-publishing and how to launch a book per month.

"Digital Retirement" is different than "28 Books to $100K" because it concentrates more on wealth, retirement, and creating your financial future using writing as the investment vehicle. It's designed to motivate and inspire you to take your financial future into your own hands and replace your Social Security income with digital income strategically.

You don't have to be at retirement age to create retirement income. If you're 30 years old and want to retire in a couple of years, you can! This book is also for people like me (I'm 56 years old) who are getting close to retirement and don't have a solid financial plan or don't have any plan.

YOUR FUTURE IS BRIGHT

I'm excited for your future and your potential to make a living with your writing and create your own social security check.

Warren Buffet is famous for saying:

"Only when the tide goes out do you discover who's been swimming naked."

I was swimming naked for years because my only retirement plan was Social Security and my now depleted 401K account. I've taken back my power and am creating my financial future and destiny through *Digital Retirement*.

If you're ready to retire early, create passive income, and enjoy more freedom than you ever have before… let's get started!

FREE GIFT FOR MY READERS

Join my private Facebook group along with hundreds of other authors who want to write a book a month to create passive, recurring income and retire early.

To join, visit: **Facebook.com/groups/28BooksTo100K**

Members of the Facebook group have access to my free templates, including:

- **Rapid Writing Secrets**
- **Annual Publishing Chart**
- **Book Creation Template**
- **Income Tracker**
- **And More!**

I want you to have the tools you need to achieve the same results I have.

CHAPTER 1:
THE RETIREMENT CRISIS

Contributed by Retirement Expert Daniel Rondberg

"Assets can be lost, they can be swindled, they can be divorced, they can be sued. Income is the secret to a successful retirement."
~ Tom Hegna

The most important thing I've learned about retirement after contributing as a blog writer for the number one economist in the world on the subject of retirement is this:

Retirement is all about income, not assets.

Everyone struggles with this because our entire working life, we are taught to focus on growing our net worth and trying to reach "millionaire status." In financial terms, this is known as the *accumulation phase*.

Retirement is the *deaccumulation phase* where you spend down those assets. I tell clients to think of it like farming – first, you plant and grow the crops, and then you harvest them.

This is why responses to AARP's annual survey every year indicate that the #1 fear amongst seniors is not dying—it is running out of money.

The truth is no one really *runs out of money*; they run out of their *standard of living*.

Social Security provides a monthly check forever but when a retiree's assets are gone, a shortfall is created between what they need to live on and their monthly Social Security check. This is such a common problem today that the top economists coast to coast agree we are sitting on the verge of a *Retirement Crisis.*

The *Retirement Crisis* is a big issue, and it is just the beginning.

According to the 2019 Social Security Wage Statistics Report, 92% of Americans makes less than $100,000 annually. In addition, roughly 50% of Americans reach their full retirement age (FRA) with less than $25,000.

If you study these statistics throughout the years, you will notice that America's median wage of approximately $40,000 hasn't changed much since 1970, which is a huge problem in itself. But what has changed other than things getting more expensive? Why are American's struggling with retirement income at an alarming rate?

One word: Pensions

Michelle referred to "Prince Charming" in her introduction. The #1 economist, Tom Hegna, calls it something similar: "Happily Ever After."

Many retirees used to get a pension, meaning they could not manage, or should I say *mismanage*, their retirement income. Pension payments were made to them for life along with Social Security income. So, the day they retired, their income would not change and they could depend on these checks coupled with Social Security to provide income for life.

It was a great retirement strategy, but unfortunately it didn't stay this way.

In the early 1970's, Wall Street desperately wanted to manage the trillions of dollars held in pension funds. They convinced American corporations that they couldn't compete globally by providing every single employee and their spouse with a paycheck for the rest of their lives and that it was WAY more cost effective to match a 401(k) contribution than to pay for an employee's *happily ever after*. So, they lobbied Congress and passed *The Revenue Act* in 1978 which included section 401(k) and was also governed under *The Employee Retirement Income Security Act (ERISA)*.

Unfortunately, Wall Street got its way and was now able to inundate these plans with fees as high as 4%, as described in Tony Robbins book "Unshakable." Fast forward to today when these first generations of 401(k) plan participants are retiring, and what did we learn?

We learned that people either didn't save enough or only contributed enough to get their employer's match. Also, those with almost no financial education didn't know what to invest in or their investments were either way too conservative or way too risky, both having catastrophic effects on their retirement.

To make matters worse, we had no idea that the 2000's would bring the most dramatic volatility our economy has ever experienced, with low to near zero interest rates for over a decade. Also, people are living longer than ever before.

The Retirement Crisis is a big problem, and it is just the beginning. We haven't even seen what happens to these 401(k) savers if/when taxes are raised from the lowest rates in the last 80 years. Sounds pretty grim, right?

Not to worry because thanks to Michelle's message on *Digital Retirement*, retirees now have a secret weapon that no other generation has had before.

What I learned from Michelle has literally changed the way I think about retirement income forever.

Before I explain more about that, I want to share with you my background…

I have helped hundreds of people retire, and I spend a tremendous amount of time studying one thing: Retirement Income. I contribute for an economist known as the "Father of Guaranteed Lifetime Income," Tom Hegna. I spent all of 2018 traveling the country speaking to Insurance agents, financial advisors, CPAs, and attorneys on this subject. I have three international bestselling books on the subject of Retirement Income. I've also been featured in Forbes, Market Watch, Yahoo Finance, USA Today and others. I have spent nearly the last decade giving almost 100 public seminars on Social Security and Retirement Income. I qualify for the World's top association of financial advisors and insurance agents who help people with retirement called *Top of the Table* (fewer than 2300 financial professionals in the entire word qualify). I've spent tens of thousands of dollars to attend the top symposiums and lectures by economists on retirement.

I mention all of this not to brag, but to let you know that I am truly a dedicated student of Retirement Income, and I pride myself on my deeply rooted background in the fundamental principles, but I combine that with new innovative ways to help my clients.

I am constantly looking for an "edge," something that brings enormous value. What Michelle has taught me is not only a game changer, but I would argue that it must be a consideration and included in the discussion for every single retiree, and I can prove it.

Below is the average Return on Investment (ROI) you can expect from these sources:

- Stocks – 10%
- Mutual Funds – 12%
- Bonds – 3%
- CD's – 2%
- Annuities – 3%
- PPMs – 10%
- Loans – 8%
- REITS – 6%
- Rentals – 5%

Sources: Bankrate.com, Pimco.com, Finviz.com, Nerd Wallet.com

Each of these investments have different levels of risk and require varying initial deposits or even investor qualifications. However, they also pale in comparison to creating *Digital Assets* like writing books. Yes, it's true! You can realistically launch a book on Amazon for less than $1,000, and when done properly, you can potentially earn $200 per month.

One of Michelle's books, "How to Find Your Passion," is currently earning over $1000 per month! In just nine months, Michelle has created $2,300 a month in passive income for her *Digital Retirement*!

Michelle's Digital Assets strategy yields ROIs of effectively 240%.

Writing and launching a book does require a tremendous amount of time. Like the assets described above, there is a compound interest effect when you publish on Amazon, which allows you to advertise on their platform. The more books you produce, and the more advertisements you run to promote your books, the more passive income you will earn. When you factor your time in the equation, naturally, this will lower the ROI. But this ROI is modest, and like most strategies for making income, there is risk.

However, the risk is far less when compared to the amount of money it would take to produce the same income in other ways. For example:

- REITS (Real Estate Investment Trusts): ROI - 6%; Investment: $40,000; Annual Income: $2,400
- E-book: ROI - 240%; Investment: $1,000: Annual Income: $2,400

Books produce the same income with $39,000 less at risk.

As you can see, this digital arbitrage opportunity provides a superior income opportunity with significantly less time required to save that much money, and with much less risk. Never before in history could someone anywhere in the world share their life's work or their passion while sitting on their couch pressing buttons and build that into a meaningful stream of income in their retirement. If you are out of time and need a boost to your retirement income, this may be the most important book to read so you can create the income that you need for your retirement.

After a decade of studying all options for retirement income from the top economists in the world, I truly believe that writing and self-publishing books, when launched and promoted correctly, can provide you with one of the most viable options to make a meaningful difference in your retirement income.

According to US News & World Report[4], the average Social Security benefit is $1,503 per month. That can be accomplished, as Michelle demonstrates, by writing as few as eight books! You can create a lifetime of work in eight months. I have not found anything else that provides that level of income with such a low risk.

I always try everything myself before I discuss a strategy with my clients to be confident it presents an opportunity that I would incorporate into my own life. In May 2020, Michelle helped me publish my first book, "No Stone Left Unturned: How to Cash

---

[4] https://money.usnews.com/money/retirement/social-security/articles/how-much-you-will-get-from-social-security

In On This Hidden Treasure In the Tax Code," and immediately I was hooked!

Becoming a published author has truly changed my life. I've been featured in the news. My family, friends, and clients all look at me differently. People are proud of me, and it comes with a new found respect that I couldn't have predicted. It has also boosted my business, helped me obtain speaking engagements with companies that previously would not let me on their stage, and has gotten people to call me.

I previously had five websites that never received a single organic visitor. Since Michelle helped me self-publish my book, I get new visitors to all of my sites daily.

Finally, nothing fills my heart with more pride than watching my three-year-old daughter march around the house with my book in her hands as she proclaims, "This is my Daddy's book!" Needless to say, I was hooked.

Now, I write a book a month with Michelle. I have published four books in just four months and am currently on track to replace half of my earned income with the revenue from my books by the middle of 2021.

It sounds too good to be true, but I want you to know it is a lot work. Your first book will be the hardest, but once you get the first one under your belt, you will get a little better, and once you form a system (like Michelle teaches), it becomes very manageable.

I want to close with an encouraging message.

For people who say it's too hard or there isn't enough time, I want to say this. Despite my age, I am one of the least do-it-yourself and tech savvy people in their 30's. I wasn't even on Facebook until age 30. I also work about 60 hours a week in my practice. I have a company that provides marketing and education for financial professionals. I am married, and my wife and I have a three-year-old and a nine-month-old. I contribute as a blog writer for two of the largest retirement resources. Tom Hegna.com and NAIFA. I run all of the media for the company I work for. I host a podcast, write blog posts, and create YouTube videos. I run the benefits division for one of the largest real estate companies in Arizona that has over 2,000 agents. I speak at live events and I am able to write a book a month. So I promise you that if I can do it, you can too!

I'm not saying this to brag about how busy I am, but to illustrate that Michelle's system really makes this possible, even with a schedule as demanding as mine.

The power to change your future is in your hands!

CHAPTER 2: GET RICH SLOW IS A LOSING GAME

> *"The message of 'Get Rich Slow' is clear: Sacrifice your today, your dreams, and your life for a plan that pays dividends after most of your life has evaporated."*
> ~ MJ Demarco, author of "The Millionaire Fastlane"

I don't know about you, but I'm not interested in *wealth in a wheelchair*. Why sacrifice the present for a future that may come with many variables you cannot control?

Like many of us, I was taught to go to school, get a degree, get a "good job," sacrifice, settle for less, stop dreaming about financial freedom, and accept the status quo.

I did that working for 17 years as a paralegal, and I never got off the living paycheck-to-paycheck hamster wheel. In hindsight, making only $50,000 a year after working 17 years doesn't sound very smart.

I was on the slow path to wealth, or what I like to call the *NO PATH TO WEALTH.*

HOW MUCH IS ENOUGH?

There are many variables you must consider when calculating how much money you will need to retire, such as

- Age
- Pre-Tax Income
- Current Retirement Savings
- Other Savings
- Monthly Retirement Spending
- Other Expected Income
- Desired Retirement Age
- Life Expectancy
- Investment Rate of Return

I like the Retirement Calculator on Nerd Wallet[5] because you can input the numbers and get a snapshot of how much you need to retire and where you currently stand.

According to this retirement calculator, I am 58% there. Try the calculator to determine where you are right now.

They say, "What gets measured, gets managed." Just because "ignorance is bliss" doesn't mean it won't hurt you. It's time to wake up and smell the impending lifestyle change when it comes to your financial future. It's time to stop waiting for *Prince Charming* to save you.

---

[5] https://www.nerdwallet.com/investing/retirement-calculator

FUTURE DISCOUNTING

Most people don't prepare for the future because of something called *Future Discounting*.

Authors Jane B. Burk, Ph.D., and Lenora M. Yuen, Ph.D., explain more about this in their book "Procrastination: Why You Do It. What to Do About It NOW":

> "An example of an unbalanced perspective is de-emphasizing the future, which can create a problem for the present. Behavioral economists as well as social psychologists have observed that when an event or goal is far off in the future (such as funding your kids' college education or creating an adequate retirement account for yourself), it seems almost unreal, and therefore it feels less important than it might actually be. By contrast, goals that are close in time (such as getting a big screen TV for the weekend playoffs or doing your taxes on April 14) are experienced as more vivid or 'salient.' So, even if the present goal (getting the TV) is less important than the long-term goal (saving for college or retirement), people are more likely to do what's immediate rather than what's important for the future. This is called 'future discounting' and it is a part of the human experience that makes procrastination so compelling."

You read the numbers that myself and Daniel Rondberg shared which show how the majority of people are unprepared for retirement. Future discounting explains in part why we do that.

I wrote this book to remind myself and others to remove the blinders we all have on and start preparing for the future now.

$40,000 per Month In Income Created in Just 5 years

There is a great interview on YouTube[6] with author Steven Higgins, who is now making $40,000 a month from his books on Amazon; his income soared when he started writing a book a month.

At age 40, it took Steven five years to write his first book; then it took him five months to write his second book. After that, he started writing a book a month, and within three years, he was earning $40,000 a month and quit his job as an engineer last year.

He writes fiction books, so that should inspire all the fiction authors reading this. He is currently writing two books a month!

IT'S NEVER TOO LATE TO START

Let's take a look at some late starters:

- Sam Walton founded the first Walmart at age 44.
- Henry Ford was 45 when he became an entrepreneur.
- Julia Child was 49 when she launched her career and her cookbook, *Mastering the Art of French Cooking.*
- In 1954, at the age of 52, Ray Kroc became a franchising agent for McDonalds. He bought out the owners in 1961.
- Colonel Sanders (Harland Sanders) was 66 when he began to franchise his chicken business. He later sold the business for $2 million.
- Judge Judy did not start on camera until age 52.

---

[6] https://youtu.be/5zgA1f53loU

Whether you are young and want to retire early or you are planning for the future, or you're close to or at retirement age like me, it's never too late to start. If you create $2,300 a month in income like I did in just nine months, how could that money improve and enhance your life?

You'll find it doesn't have to take 35 years to create income or wealth. It's time to exit the slow path to wealth and get on the accelerated path to wealth!

MULTIPLE STREAMS OF INCOME

According to research[7], 65% of millionaires have at least three income streams, thereby diversifying their dependence on any one stream.

It's risky to rely on one source of income for your future. Over the years, I've made money in a variety of ways, such as:

- Royalties from my books
- Copywriting
- Website Design
- Search Engine Optimization (SEO)
- Coaching
- Selling Online Courses
- Bestselling Author Program (done-for-you)
- Ghostwriting
- Sales
- Affiliate Income

---

[7] https://millionairefoundry.com/millionaire-statistics/

HOW THIS ATTORNEY USED HER WRITING TO STOP TAKING PAIN IN THE A$$ CLIENTS

I serendipitously met an attorney, Lori, who attended one of my writers' retreats (Ocean Writing), and we became instant friends and business colleagues. We loved to complain about our mutual dissatisfaction with parts of the legal field and we laughed at some of the crazy stories we both had.

Lori explained that she wanted to be a ghostwriter to create a new stream of income for herself and her family. She didn't want to quit her legal practice per se, but she wanted to take on fewer "pain in the a$$" clients – the high drama, high-maintenance, soul-sucking clients.

This began our business relationship, and I am happy to say she has now ghostwritten many books for my clients in my www.bestsellingauthorprogram.com

She loves the diversity that ghostwriting books in different genres brings to her life while creating this new income stream. Now in her 40's, she is the author of four bestselling humorous books, and her kids are on their way to college as I am writing this book.

It's never too late to start creating a new financial future for yourself.

The path of least resistance is to get rich slow and wait for *Prince Charming* to save you (the guy, the girl, the Social Security check, the pension, the 401K, etc.).

The path to financial power and a brighter future begins by taking matters into your own hands, literally.

Now, let's talk about the 4 Secrets to Wealth…

CHAPTER 3:
4 SECRETS TO WEALTH

Years ago, my cousin's husband invited me to be part of a network marketing company. I was very excited because I truly believed this was my ticket to wealth. I attended every meeting and quickly rose up in the organization to lead meetings and recruit others.

I had an organization with hundreds of people in it, but that wasn't reflected in my monthly check. I figured it would catch up sooner or later.

A top executive in the company spoke at one of my meetings, and his speech went something like this:

> "You're building this amazing organization on Earth now, and when you move up to the next level, you leave Earth and go to Mars to start a new organization."

What?!

I called my business partner and told him what I *thought* I heard – that everything we had been building for the last year was for the person above me, and once I moved to the next level, this person (my cousin's husband) would **Get. It. All.**

My business partner thought I must be mistaken because he pointed out, "That would be insane."

Guess what?

It was both true and insane. I had worked day and night building my team to create residual income and wealth for me and my family, but after a year of work, I had nothing.

WEALTH SECRET #1: OWN THE VEHICLE

You must own the vehicle you are using to build wealth. I know many network marketing companies are very seductive, but I also have a lot of inside information that has proven to me it's not worth the time to build an income that can be taken away from you at any moment by the company who has all the power and control to change the compensation plan.

Some network marketing companies count on unsuspecting people that don't fully understand the compensation plan to build their company.

Moreover, how many times have you heard about business partnerships ending up in legal battles leaving the owners nothing after spending all their money on attorney's fees? Having been a paralegal for 17 years, I know this is very common.

When you write a book, you own the copyright and the rights to the royalties that come in every month. Even if you hire a ghostwriter, you own the book. The ghostwriter is paid for providing a service and has no rights to future income. Of course, you want to have a good contract if you do engage a ghostwriter so that it is clear you and you alone own the work.

You must rely on yourself 100% and not put your trust in *Prince Charming* — a business partner, network marketing company, or anyone else you rely on for income and wealth.

WEALTH SECRET #2: PRODUCERS GET RICH

There are two types of people in this world—consumers and creators.

Which one are you?

I have always loved learning, and it is common for me to read one or two books a week, which is more than 100 books per year. I also love attending webinars, summits, and other virtual events to learn different aspects of business. Additionally, I enjoy listening to podcasts and attending in-person events and workshops.

I'll always be a lifelong learner, and I do believe that *learners are earners*.

But there came a point in my business and my life when I had to learn to pull back on "consuming" other people's materials and start creating my own.

I still am an avid reader, but now I produce as much as I consume.

That's right. If you want to get rich, you must become a content producer.

In his book "One Million Followers," Brendan Kane says:

> "If you have something to offer – whether your talents are related to music, art, acting, sports, or even building a brand or start-up – and you know how to leverage digital and social platforms, you can reach millions, if not

hundreds of millions, of people around the world in no time. It's how social influencers have taken off and in some cases even become bigger than mainstream celebrities in just a matter of years. They started at home by turning on a camera and speaking to it, sharing what it is that makes them unique. With the right strategies, nearly anyone can build a massive global audience."

We are living in an incredible world right now with the power of technology at our fingertips. Notice what Brendan said, "They started at home by turning on a camera and speaking to it."

In the old days, when I was growing up, if you had a business you wanted to advertise, you had to invest a lot of money by taking out ads in the local newspapers, the *Yellow Pages*, or hiring a film crew to do a commercial.

Today, the barrier to entry is low. Anyone with an internet connection, a computer, and a camera can create content in the form of blogs, vlogs, articles, YouTube videos, Facebook lives, etc. You have the power to create and produce anything you want.

In this case, we are talking about creating and producing books without a publisher (self-publishing).

Think back to pre-Amazon when you had to write a detailed book proposal and send it out to dozens or hundreds of literary agents who were the gatekeepers to the publishing houses. The majority of books were rejected and authors' dreams were crushed.

Now we can write and publish a book in a long weekend. I actually have written a book in three days.

WEALTH SECRET #3: TIME IS THE QUEEN OF ALL ASSETS

Time is a finite and valuable resource that we can't replenish, no matter how wealthy we become.

As you learn to become a "producer" and "creator," you will realize how important your time is, and you will protect it with your life.

For years, I gave away my time to others in my business for very little in return. There's a term for this — "Under-earning." One sign that you are an under-earner is that you give away your time for free or you don't charge enough.

If you want to write a book a month, you must absolutely learn to protect your time.

I heard a famous model once say that she doesn't get out of bed for less than $10,000. That inspired me to keep raising my prices, and I've learned higher prices attract lower-maintenance clients (fewer complaints, fewer questions, and less demands on your time)!

And I absolutely love these types of clients. They are typically business people who understand what it takes to run a business and don't have unreasonable demands. With one client per month, I have a six-figure business. With two clients per month, I have a multiple six-figure business.

Because I charge more now, I have more free time to spend however I wish.

I made a commitment in January 2020 to write a book a month, and I now have the time to do it. My goal is to make six figures in passive income in the next 18-24 months with my books and courses.

Protect your time. Don't give it away in the name of being of service because broke people are rarely of service to anyone since they are always worried about money.

WEALTH SECRET #4: FOCUSED ATTENTION

FOCUS is one of the most valuable skills in business, and is becoming increasingly rare. If you can master this skill, you'll achieve extraordinary results and make more money than most people.

In his book, "Deep Work: Rules for Focused Success In a Distracted World," Cal Newport says:

> "Deep work is the ability to focus without distraction on a cognitively demanding task. It's a skill that allows you to quickly master complicated information and produce better results in less time. Deep work will make you better at what you do and provide the sense of true fulfillment that comes from craftsmanship. In short, deep work is like a super power in our increasingly competitive twenty-first century economy. And yet, most people have lost the ability to go deep – spending their days instead in a frantic blur of email and social media, not even realizing there's a better way."

When I started writing a book a month, I have to admit, it was challenging. I quickly realized I had a focus problem.

Coincidentally, I attended a book festival and picked up a book by Catherine Price, "How to Break Up With Your Phone," and discovered my life was being sucked away one text message, one social media post, and one email at a time.

If I wanted to write a book a month, I needed to get my life and my time back.

I read Catherine's book, and the following especially resonated with me:

"Today, just over a decade since smartphones entered our lives, we're beginning to suspect that their impact on our lives might not be entirely good. We feel busy but ineffective... The same technology that gives us freedom can also act like a leash—and the more tethered we become, the more it raises the question of who's actually in control."

I had lost control of my time and my ability to focus. It wasn't an overnight event, it was a slow, insidious change that happened over a long period of time.

Below are some other interesting statistics from Price's book:

- Americans check their phones 47 times per day. For people between 18 and 24, the average is 82. Collectively, this adds up to more than 9 billion phone checks every day.

- On average, Americans spend more than 4 hours a day on their phones. That amounts to about 28 hours a week, 112 hours a month, or 56 full days a year.

> *"Whenever you check for a new post on Instagram or whenever you go on the New York Times to see if there's a new thing, it's not even about the content. It's just about seeing a new thing. You get addicted to that feeling."*
> *~Aziz Ansari*

Most of us are addicted to our phones, social media, email, and technology.

I actually bought Catherine's book for my kids, and after reading it, I realized I was the one who needed it.

In his books, "Irresistible: The Rise of Addictive Technology" and the "Business of Keeping us Hooked," Adam Alter says,

> "Just as drugs have become more powerful over time, so has the thrill of behavioral feedback. Product designers are smarter than ever. They know how to push our buttons and how to encourage us to use their products not just once but over and over."

If you want to write a book a month, one that has substance and meaning, you need to claim back your time, attention, and ability to focus.

In "Deep Work," Cal Newport says there are two core abilities for thriving in the new economy and they are:

- The ability to master hard things.
- The ability to produce at an elite level, in terms of both quality and speed.

Even if you are talented and skilled, if you don't produce, you won't thrive.

The only way to *produce* is to remove the shallow concerns from your life and build up your muscle of focused attention.

Roy Baumeister wrote:

> *"You have a finite amount of willpower that becomes depleted as you use it."*

If I wake up and start my day doing yoga, meditating, reading books, taking a walk, eating breakfast, checking emails, doing client work, talking on the phone, or scrolling through social media, there is 99.9% chance that I won't get around to do my writing.

Now that I've been writing a book a month for nine months, I've realized that good intentions mean absolutely nothing. I must do my writing first thing in the morning before anything else, and I must do it in my pajamas!

Why do I have to write in my pajamas?

Because the temptation to go out to Starbucks or run errands once I am showered and dressed is too great. So, I have to trick myself and stay in my pajamas to write so I can achieve my goals. After I've completed my writing for the day, I reward myself by doing these other things.

It's been hard retraining myself and my habits. So much so that I wrote a book last month called "Spandex Habits" where I detail how to create flexible habits that fit into your life as well as how to reverse and remove bad habits.

Cheryl Richardson, an author and Life Coach, once said, "A high quality life has more to do with what you remove from it than what you add to it."

What do you need to remove from your life to make time for the focused attention and deep work required to write a book a month?

Neal Stephenson, a science fiction writer, explains it very well:

"The productivity equation is a non-linear one, in other words. This accounts for why I am a bad correspondent and why I very rarely accept speaking engagements. If I organize my life in such a way that I get lots of long, consecutive, uninterrupted time-chunks, I can write novels. But as those chunks get separated and fragmented, my productivity as a novelist drops spectacularly."

So, you have a choice – you can write a book a month and create your *Digital Retirement* – or you can answer a lot of emails, text messages, and engage in endless scrolling on social media.

Which one do you choose?

I've had to eliminate many things in my life to make time to write a book a month, such as watching television, checking social media, and reading unlimited amounts of books. I've learned to make my writing a priority and give myself an abundance of uninterrupted, undistracted, and focused time.

Everyone's life is different, and we all have different responsibilities and obligations, but here are three ways you can add more focused time to your life:

1. Give yourself one day a week to do your writing and deep work (or you could do an entire weekend).
2. Give yourself a 1-4 hours per day of uninterrupted, focused work – mornings are best for me. One of my clients, a busy psychologist, has written six novels, and he writes every night from 10 p.m. to 2 a.m. Do whatever works best for you.
3. Give yourself focused time whenever you can find it – this method is great if you can instantly switch to deep work.

I'll end this chapter with this story of a man who needed to write his book, but couldn't find the "uninterrupted" time required. So, he booked a round-trip, business class ticket to Tokyo, and wrote during the entire flight to and from Japan, drinking an espresso in the lounge once he arrived in Japan. He finished his manuscript during the 30-hour trip.

If there's a will, there's a way.

Remember, we have limited and finite willpower, so once that's used up, then you can do all those other shallow activities that don't require deep cognitive thinking.

Next, I want to talk about shortcuts to success...

CHAPTER 4:
SHORTCUTS TO SUCCESS

"Everything popular is wrong."
~ Oscar Wilde, The Importance of Being Earnest

SHORTCUT TO SUCCESS #1 –
LEARN TO SEPARATE TIME FROM INCOME

In "The 4-Hour Workweek," author Timothy Ferriss says,

"Our goal is simple: to create an automated vehicle for generating cash without consuming time. That's it… So first things first: cash flow and time. With these two currencies, all other things are possible. Without them, nothing is possible."

DO THE WORK ONCE AND GET PAID OVER AND OVER

I started www.becomea6figurewoman.com, my first online business, in 2005 because I was having a hard time filling seats for live workshops that I was had been doing at adult education centers, community colleges, Unity church, and other local venues. I decided instead to package up my content and sell it online.

I hired someone to build my website, and in the first 30 days, I made over $2,500 selling a $197 course. I was hooked on doing the work once and getting paid over and over.

I was so accustomed to trading dollars for hours in the legal field; this was a new and refreshing way to make money. I didn't mind putting in the work up front, as long as I could continually make money from that work.

I sold online courses until 2011, when I began doing website design, copywriting, and Search Engine Optimization (SEO). Selling these services was great experience, and I'm glad I learned these skills, but this was not a business I could scale, and I was also not creating "passive" income. Doing website design was equivalent to trading dollars for hours.

In 2014, I shut down the website design business to focus on my www.bestsellingauthorprogram.com business, which I built to multiple six figures in a few years doing mostly "done-for-you" services. Again, I was not creating passive income. It's great income, don't get me wrong, and I'm not complaining, but there was still something missing in my financial future.

If I stop working, I have no income.

Making six figures online is great – I have time and money freedom, but if I stop working, I have no income. My business depends 100% on me even though I have a small team to take a client from unpublished author to #1 bestselling author in 12 weeks. There is a lot of work on the back end because I have many done-for-you services included in my packages.

Now, you might be wondering, "Michelle, why don't you just sell a course for your bestseller program?"

Great question.

I actually do have online courses for people who want to do it themselves.

Right now, as I'm writing this book, I still have done-for-you services, however, as I increase my passive income, I will be shutting down many of those done-for-you services to give myself more time to focus on creating passive income.

MY SHORTCUT TO WEALTH: WRITING A BOOK A MONTH

My background in the legal field where I did a lot of research and writing, coupled with my experience as a newspaper reporter, copywriter, and blogger, have given me the skills needed to write a book a month.

Other skills required to write and publish a book a month include:

- Editing
- Formatting your book for eBook and print
- Publishing on Amazon
- Cover Design
- Category and Keyword Research
- Writing Book Descriptions
- Launching Books to the #1 Bestsellers Lists

Since this has been my business for the past seven years, I have a team to do this month after month.

I want to stress to you that if you don't have the skillset above, that's okay. You can learn to outsource tasks and still achieve your goals. In fact, to be successful, you should outsource.

SHORTCUT TO SUCCESS #2: OUTSOURCING

"A man is rich in proportion to the number of things he can afford to let alone."
~ Henry David Thoreau

Creating a shortcut to wealth involves working smarter and building a system to replace yourself; something I failed to do for the past seven years.

A ONE-WOMAN SHOW

When I started my bestselling author program, I didn't have the money to outsource at first, so I invested heavily in learning the skillset to do *everything* in my business. I was a one-woman show, like the guy behind the curtain in *The Wizard of Oz*. I did it all — editing, formatting, cover design, graphics, category and keyword research, writing book descriptions, publishing on Amazon and of course, doing book launches.

Honestly, it was exhausting!

You don't have to learn everything, unless you have the time and desire to do so, but my advice is to outsource your weaknesses and focus on your strengths.

We are going to go deeper into what types of books you can write and why you should only write short books. Understand this: everything in this process can be outsourced. I have included a list of valuable Resources at the end of this book that you can use to outsource the steps involved in this process, especially if you have a low budget.

I'm quite surprised when people who want to write books have a ZERO budget for their projects.

Many publishing companies invest a minimum of $25,000 to $35,000 for every client and book they take on.

If you want a business that will create passive income, then yes, you will have to invest money in this business. It doesn't have to be thousands of dollars, but you must publish a high-quality, professional book with a unique hook and message if you want to be successful.

The quickest path to building a *Digital Retirement* is to write a book a month. I mentioned in the Introduction that I have created $2,300 in passive income in nine months! I've already exceeded what I will receive from my Social Security 6-10 years from now.

In a later chapter, I'll lay out exactly how to write a book a month, but right now I want to talk about writing your first book with a unique message so you don't get lost in the crowd.

IT TAKES MORE THAN IDEAS TO BE SUCCESSFUL

I have bad news for you – ideas are not enough when it comes to writing and publishing books. In fact, ideas are the easy part; they are a dime a dozen.

This is the part that cannot be outsourced, you can't hire someone to come up with a great idea for you.

In "Perennial Seller: The Art of Making and Marketing Work That Lasts," author Ryan Holiday says:

> "The first step of any creator hoping for lasting success – whether for ten years or ten centuries – is to accept that hope has nothing to do with it. To be great, one must make great work, and making great work is incredibly hard. It must be our primary focus. We must set out, from the beginning, with complete and total commitment to the idea that our best chance for success starts during the creative process."

PUTTING YOUR BEST FOOT FORWARD

The publishing field changed dramatically when Amazon's self-publishing platform, Kindle Direct Publishing (KDP), came along. Prior to KDP, there were numerous gatekeepers that prevented people from becoming a published author. Now, with a few clicks on the computer, anyone, just about anywhere in the world, can self-publish their books.

That being said, there are a lot of crappy books on Amazon.

If you write books that make a difference and change people's lives, and put out the best product you can, you will stack the odds in your favor.

On the other hand, if you take the path of least resistance to make a quick buck, you will not have long-term success. Every book you write must begin with the right intent – a deeper purpose and meaning.

I write books because I'm passionate about helping others have more time and money freedom in their lives. I've been in JOB prison before and I remember how painful it was. I've also lived paycheck-to-paycheck, and it's not a fun way to live. I love writing books that have the power to transform someone's life – just like so many books have transformed my own life.

In the next chapter, I will share with you some brainstorming techniques to help you write a great book that people want to read.

CHAPTER 5:
HOW TO AVOID WRITING CRAPPY BOOKS

I believe that the more you write, the better your writing will become. A lot of great writers started out as mediocre writers. Also keep in mind that good editors can take a mediocre book and make it great.

If you feel in your heart that writing isn't your strong suit or you really hate writing, but have something compelling to share with others, then you can hire a ghostwriter to write your book.

You could also speak your book and record yourself. I recommend using an app like REV and then have it transcribed by them to create your book.

Just remember, a great book is not written during a single episode of genius; instead, it is made piece-by-piece. That is the creative process, but it all begins with an idea.

Millions of books are self-published each year, so it's getting harder and harder to stand out.

It's not difficult to write a book *we want to write*; however, it is difficult to write a book other people not only want, but need.

Most writers start writing what they want to write without doing the prework, which is market research.

Lawyers wouldn't show up for a court case in front of the Judge without doing "discovery," which consists of things like Interrogatories, Request for Production of Documents, Depositions of expert witnesses, etc.

Doing the prework and coming up with your unique topic and hook is the most important thing to do besides actually writing your book.

I'm a big fan of Ryan Holiday who is a brilliant author who has many successful and bestselling books like:

- *The Obstacle is the Way*
- *Stillness is the Key*
- *Ego is the Enemy*
- *The Daily Stoic*
- *Trust Me, I'm Lying*
- *Lives of the Stoics*
- *Growth Hacker Marketing*
- *Perennial Seller*

I've read several of his books, and I can tell he spends a great deal of time on the pre-work to develop unique ideas for his books.

So, how does one come up with an idea for a unique, creative, and in-demand book?

QUESTIONS ARE THE ANSWER

Holiday suggests that any project creator should answer these questions:

- What does this teach?
- What does this solve?
- How am I entertaining?
- What am I giving?
- What are we offering?
- What are we sharing?

In essence, the bigger question is: *What will people pay for?* If you don't know the answer, or if the answer isn't overwhelming, keep thinking.

In their bestselling book, "Blue Ocean Strategy," authors W. Chan Kim and Renee Mauborgne, suggest that instead of battling numerous competitors in a contested "red ocean," it is far better to seek fresh, uncontested, "blue water."

WHAT'S YOUR BLUE OCEAN IDEA FOR A BOOK?

Holiday has four additional questions that can take your book to the next level:

1. What sacred cows am I slaying?
2. What dominant institution am I displacing?
3. What groups am I disrupting?
4. What people am I pissing off?

You need a dose of audaciousness to avoid writing crappy books. This is not the time to be subtle. Ryan warns:

> "Stuff that's boring now is probably going to be boring in twenty years."

In my *Rapid Writing Secrets* (which you can get for FREE when you join my Facebook group), I talk about some ways to create a unique hook. Here's an excerpt from that training:

THE SNOWFLAKE HOOK

No two snowflakes are the same. You must write a book that has NOT been written before. How, you ask? Here are some ideas (with actual book titles as examples):

- **Change the Perspective**: "Public Speaking for People Who Hate Public Speaking"
- **Shock Factor**: "The Subtle Art of Not Giving a F*ck"
- **Create a New Process/Method/System**: "Habit Stacking: 127 Small Changes to Improve Your Health, Wealth and Happiness"
- **Make the Complicated Simple**: "The Index Card: Why Personal Finance Doesn't Have to Be Complicated"
- **Against the Norm**: "The 30-Hour Day: Develop Achiever's Mindset and Habits"
- **Contrary Messaging**: "The Obstacle is the Way"
- **Solve a Million Dollar Problem**: "Profit First: Transform Your Business from a Cash-Eating Monster to a Money-Making Machine"
- **Mimic the Classics**: "Write and Grow Rich"

A good hook grabs attention and piques interest! You've got to train yourself to think outside the box.

There is nothing new under the sun, but you can always put your unique spin on it, add your original story to it, or combine two unrelated things to come up with something completely unprecedented!

THREE PILLARS TO FIND A BOOK TOPIC

Now that you know how NOT to write a crappy book, let's explore what you can write about.

We all have experiences, ideas, skills, obstacles we've overcome, lessons we've learned in life, and that's why I believe everyone has a book in them. In fact, everyone has multiple books inside of them. Even if you don't consider yourself a writer, you have something to share with others.

I wrote about the three pillars of creating an online course in my book, "Make Money While You Sleep," and you can use those same pillars to determine what you should write books about:

- **PILLAR ONE: SCARY TIMES SKILLS** – Life challenges, struggles, and obstacles that you have overcome.
- **PILLAR TWO: JOB AUTOPSY** – Your skills, talents, and expertise that you enjoy and/or others say you are good at.
- **PILLAR THREE: THE CURIOSITY MAP** – Identifying your curiosities and following the bread crumb trail. You are probably an expert at many things, but you just don't realize it!

Below are some questions to get you thinking of topics for your books.

PILLAR ONE: SCARY TIMES SKILLS

MEMORY JOGGER #1

What challenges, struggles, or obstacles have you overcome in your life that might position you to help others in a similar situation?

Don't over-complicate this exercise. Think about PIVOTAL MOMENTS in your life that you could possibly teach others.

Examples: Have you overcome a financial situation, a health crisis, a relationship problem, a spiritual awakening, a career shift, a family challenge, an affair, an abusive relationship, etc.?

Below, list any significant obstacles that you have successfully navigated through and come out on the other side.

_____
_____
_____
_____
_____
_____
_____
_____
_____
_____
_____

MEMORY JOGGER #2

Write 1-10 sentences describing how you overcame these challenges, struggles, or obstacles. What results did you achieve by working through the challenges?

_____
_____
_____
_____
_____
_____
_____
_____
_____
_____
_____
_____
_____
_____
_____
_____
_____
_____
_____
_____
_____
_____
_____
_____
_____

MEMORY JOGGER #3

When you think about a difficult situation, what help or resources do you wish you had so you could more easily work through the process?

_____
_____
_____
_____
_____
_____
_____
_____
_____
_____
_____
_____
_____
_____
_____
_____
_____
_____
_____
_____
_____
_____
_____
_____
_____

MEMORY JOGGER #4

Describe the pain you felt about the situation. Give as many details and use as many feeling words as you can. Be honest about how bad you felt and your pain level at the time.

_____
_____
_____
_____
_____
_____
_____
_____
_____
_____
_____
_____
_____
_____
_____
_____
_____
_____
_____
_____
_____
_____
_____
_____

MEMORY JOGGER #5

When you reflect on the amount of pain, how much would you have paid to resolve it?

MEMORY JOGGER #6

What skills and knowledge did you acquire during this challenging time?

_____

MEMORY JOGGER #7

How can you use what you learned to help others in a similar situation?

_____
_____
_____
_____
_____
_____
_____
_____
_____
_____
_____
_____
_____
_____
_____
_____
_____
_____
_____
_____
_____
_____
_____
_____
_____

PILLAR TWO: JOB AUTOPSY

MEMORY JOGGER #1

- Job Title
- Job Tasks
- Task rating on a scale of 1-10. (1 – Hated to 10 – Loved)

Example:

Job Title: Paralegal

Tasks and Ratings:

1. Writing pleadings – 10
2. Legal Research – 10
3. Editing documents – 3
4. Filing – 1
5. Answering the telephone – 1
6. Making copies – 1
7. Interviewing Clients – 10
8. Typing on the computer – 8
9. Going to Court – 10

The goal is to see which tasks you find joy in doing and potentially write your book around this high-passion skillset. If you excel at a specific skill but find no pleasure doing it, you would not want to create a book based on that topic.

If you've been working long enough, you have skills that others want to learn.

Now it's time to explore the jobs you've had. For each job, list the job title, job tasks, and rate each task.

JOB 1

Job Title: _____

List all the tasks you performed in this job and rate each one from 1-10 (1 – HATED to 10 – LOVED).

- _____
- _____
- _____
- _____
- _____
- _____
- _____
- _____
- _____
- _____

JOB 2

Job Title: _____

List all the tasks you performed in this job and rate each one from 1-10 (1 – HATED to 10 – LOVED).

- _____
- _____
- _____
- _____
- _____
- _____
- _____
- _____
- _____
- _____

JOB 3

Job Title: _____

List all the tasks you performed in this job and rate each one from 1-10 (1 – HATED to 10 – LOVED).

- _____
- _____
- _____
- _____
- _____
- _____
- _____
- _____
- _____
- _____

JOB 4

Job Title: _____

List all the tasks you performed in this job and rate each one from 1-10 (1 – HATED to 10 – LOVED).

- _____
- _____
- _____
- _____
- _____
- _____
- _____
- _____
- _____
- _____

JOB 5

Job Title: _____

List all the tasks you performed in this job and rate each one from 1-10 (1 – HATED to 10 – LOVED).

- _____
- _____
- _____
- _____
- _____
- _____
- _____
- _____
- _____
- _____

NOTE: If you have your own business and don't have a "job," think about what tasks you are frequently asked to do. If you are successful in your business, others will ask you for help; this is how many of my book ideas were born.

What aspects of your business do people ask you for help doing?

___

MEMORY JOGGER #2

Using the information from the job autopsy above, list the tasks you gave a rating of 7 or higher. How could you use your current or past work experience to write a book using these skills?

___

PILLAR 3: THE CURIOSITY MAP

Next up is another method to help you find a topic for your book using a *breadcrumb trail* of your curiosities. Here's what we'll be exploring:

- Podcasts you listen to
- Books you like to read
- YouTube videos you watch
- Webinars you enjoy
- Magazines you read
- What you talk about in your spare time
- Your hobbies
- Your certifications and extracurricular activities

MEMORY JOGGER #1

List the last 5-10 books that got you excited. Next to each title, explain why you love it.

_____
_____
_____
_____
_____
_____
_____
_____

MEMORY JOGGER #2

List the last 5-10 podcasts that got you excited. Next to each one, explain why you love it.

_____
_____
_____
_____
_____
_____
_____
_____
_____
_____
_____

MEMORY JOGGER #3

List the last 5-10 magazines that got you excited. Next to each one, explain why you love it.

_____
_____
_____
_____
_____
_____
_____
_____
_____
_____

MEMORY JOGGER #4

Do you have an obsession or something you talk about regularly? If so, describe it below:

_____
_____
_____
_____
_____
_____
_____
_____
_____
_____
_____

MEMORY JOGGER #5

Name your favorite 5-10 hobbies and explain why you love each one.

_____
_____
_____
_____
_____
_____
_____
_____
_____
_____
_____

MEMORY JOGGER #6

List your certifications or extracurricular activities you enjoy.

_____
_____
_____
_____
_____
_____
_____
_____

Great job doing this work! Now it's time to PUT ALL THE PUZZLE PIECES TOGETHER.

Consider your answers from the 3 Pillars above. For each Pillar, select one topic that gets your juices flowing:

PILLAR #1 TOPIC (Obstacles and Struggles)

_____

PILLAR #2 TOPIC (Job Autopsy)

_____

PILLAR #3 TOPIC (Curiosities)

_____

EXTRA

If you are self-employed, what services do you provide or what things do clients constantly ask you to help them with?

_____

It's important to find something you are passionate about and, of course, that helps others. Please take a few moments to answer the following questions:

1. What topic from the three choices above do you feel most strongly could help others?
   _____

2. In what areas do you feel you are a true expert?
   _____

3. What type of person would benefit the most from this book? Where are they in their life (probably somewhere you have been in your past)?
   _____

After completing these exercises, you should have some great ideas for your first book. This is huge! Be proud of yourself for exploring, documenting, and observing where your energy and passion flows.

Sleep on it, meditate on it, or pray about it if you like, and then go with the one topic/idea that you have the most energy around. Of course, we will need to validate your idea before you create it to ensure it's in demand.

The #1 topic for my book is: _____.

Next, we'll niche down on this topic even further to create a magnetic and working title for your book.

CHAPTER 6: REVERSE-ENGINEERING YOUR BESTSELLER

While I can't be in person or on a zoom call to help you come up with your first book title, I can help you take the steps to create a magnetic and working title for your first book.

In the previous chapter, you did the work by answering different questions and discovering what topic you want to write about.

Now, it's time to research your topic to make sure it's what I call a *high-profit topic*.

ENGLISH COTTAGE GARDENS WAS NOT A HIGH-PROFIT TOPIC

I received a strategy session application a while back from a nice couple in California who wanted to write a book about English Cottage Gardens. We had a lovely conversation, and I told them I would research the topic and get back to them.

It seemed like a good topic, but I had never done a book for a client in this genre, so I needed to do my research. I believe in data more than guessing.

I use Publisher Rocket for all of my research. It's paid software, but it will save you a lot of money because it will help you write a high-profit book rather than a low-profit book.

My research on Publisher Rocket revealed few searches for this topic:

Keywords	Number of Searches per month on Amazon
English cottage gardens	Less than 100
English cottage gardens books	Less than 100
English cottage garden	Less than 100
Cottage garden ideas	Less than 100
Cottage garden flowers	Less than 100

Additionally, *English Cottage Gardens* books on Amazon were not making much money either (I used KDSpy to get the sales numbers).

Now, these were very nice people and I could have signed them up into my high-ticket program and let them write a book on English Cottage Gardens (an area in which they were experts), but I don't take on clients unless I feel strongly that they have a high-profit topic that can be positioned correctly that will do well.

I suggested to these potential clients that they instead write a book on *raised bed and container gardening*, as I discovered during my research, this was a very hot and high-profit topic.

My research on Publisher Rocket revealed there were many more searches for this topic:

Keywords	Number of Searches per month on Amazon
Raised bed gardening books	1,161
Raised bed gardening containers	493
Container gardening book	548
Gardening in containers	626
Gardening for beginners	540
Vegetable gardening for beginners	848
Gardening for beginners herbs	849

These are much better numbers and results. Moreover, I found books on this topic making $25,000 per month. I was pleasantly surprised!

The potential clients agreed to write a book on raised bed and container gardening. Consequently, I took them on as clients and 12 weeks later, we are about to publish their brand new gardening book, which I know is going to do well!

WHY DO I KNOW THAT?

Right now, more than ever, people are worried about the food supply, and many people are interested in growing their own gardens, especially in small spaces. Also, during our market research, we read the bad reviews for the top bestselling books on Amazon and made notes on the complaints other readers had.

Using this information, they were careful to create a book that avoided most of those issues.

Essentially, we reverse-engineered a bestselling book!

10 Steps To Writing Your Bestselling Book

1. **Decide on your topic using the 3 pillars** – Go broad and go broke, or niche and grow rich. For example, if you were going to write a book on public speaking you could niche down by writing a book for a specific audience – doctors, lawyers, coaches, introverts, writers, etc.

2. **Invest in Publisher Rocket** – Research keywords that you think people will enter when searching for books on your topic. Record this information in a document and save it. After you write your book, you will use your top 7 keywords when publishing it.

3. **Check out the Competition** – After you find your keywords in Publisher Rocket, click on the green button to the right of the keyword results labeled "Competition" to view the top-selling books on that topic.

   Note: There are two ways you can find out how many

copies a book has sold. I use KDSpy and it shows me the exact number of sales in the past 30 days for eBook and print book. Or, you can look at the book's *sales ranking*, which can be found in the Product Details section of the book page on Amazon. Write down the sales ranking and then go to the free Sales Rank Calculator provided by the founder of Publisher Rocket, Dave Chesson: https://kindlepreneur.com/amazon-kdp-sales-rank-calculator/ to see the number of books that were sold to achieve that ranking.

4. **Do your Keyword Research** - When using Publisher Rocket, it will show you how many people are searching for keywords on Amazon. That is valuable information. My suggestion is if you have keywords that have a minimum of 500+ searches per month, that could be a good topic to write about. I like to look up 7 keyword phrases that have in the range of 500-2000+ searches per month on Amazon; this is my criteria. Additionally, when you look at actual books in your genre on Amazon, make sure they are making at least $1,000+ per month. This way you can assure you have a high-profit topic.

5. **Check out the bad reviews of your competition** - Review the bad reviews of the top selling books in your genre; and makes notes on ways you can improve on those complaints with your book. I've even come up with ideas for books from reading bad reviews!

6. **Browse the Table of Contents from other bestselling books** – if your book has good profit potential at this

point, review the table of contents of other books to get some ideas for writing and positioning your book.

*Did you know that you cannot copyright a book title? You could write a book right now and use the title "7 Habits of Highly Successful People." In fact, many authors use successful titles as a springboard for their own titles. For example, "Write and Grow Rich" is a take-off of Napoleon Hill's "Think and Grow Rich."

7. **Look on Reddit** – Search for posts on your topic that have a lot of engagement as well as high volume groups. You could also do this on platforms like Facebook, LinkedIn, Instagram, etc.

8. **Go to YouTube and look to see if there are any TED Talks on your topic**. Try to find ones that have a high number of views and maybe use a similar title.

9. **Poll Your Target Audience**. If you have an email list, Facebook, or other social media group, you can do a poll and ask your target audience. If you ask people outside of your target audience, you won't get accurate results.

10. **Create Several Titles and Run a Poll to Pick the Best.** Once you come up with several potential titles for your book, use https://www.surveymonkey.com/ (which is free) to see what your audience prefers. If you want a paid option for polls on cover designs or titles, go to: https://www.pickfu.com/blog/testing-book-titles-covers/

Read the article at the link below for ideas on coming up with a title for your book: https://kindlepreneur.com/how-to-title-a-book-with-good-book-titles/

Now that you've done the prework and come up with great ideas for your book…

Write down the Top 10 titles for your first book:

1. _____
2. _____
3. _____
4. _____
5. _____
6. _____
7. _____
8. _____
9. _____
10. _____

Once you've done your research and selected your title, you can use my *Book Creation Template* (which I give away in my free Facebook group) to outline your book.

First, before I fill this out, I do a mind dump on the topic and write down everything I can think of regarding this book title on post-it notes. Then I group the Post-it notes by related topics and create a working outline for my book using this information.

Book Creation Template

Book-A-Month (BAM) Book Creation Template

Book	Chapter Title	Purpose of Chapter	Subchapter 1	Subchapter 2	Subchapter 3	Subchapter 4	Subchapter 5	Subchapter 6

I like using this *Book Creation Template* because once you fill in the blanks, you have a plan that will guide you as you write your book.

I've done books without an outline, and I can tell you it makes the process much more difficult and time-consuming.

Take the time to fill out the *Book Creation Template* for every book you write.

Book Creation Template for "28 Books to $100k"

Book-A-Month (BAM) Book Creation Template

Chapter Title	Purpose of Chapter	Sub Chp. 1	Sub Chp. 2	Sub Chp. 3	Sub Chp. 4
Why Shorter is Better	The ROI is higher when you spend less time and write shorter books				
Titles, Titles, Everywhere	A title can make or break your book. Start looking around now.				
Rapid Writing Secrets	How to go from writer's block to writing a book in 14 days				
From Mind Dump to Book Outline	How to outline your book with a mind dump				
Seven Questions to Ask Before You Write Your Book	Helps you get clarity on your book				
The Bestseller Checklist	It's not enough to publish a book, you must be a bestseller				
Your 12-Month Plan	Plan your year out				
Self-Publishing 101	How to publish the right way for the highest success rate.				
Launch Like a Pro	Don't just publish your book, launch your book.				
Extra Rocket Fuel for Your Book	Amazon ads are critical to your success				
Income Goals and Income Tracking Chart	Set your goals and then track them.				
The 30-Day Roadmap to Writing a Book	Your 30-day plan for success				

Remember, the purpose of a non-fiction book is to take the reader from one side of the river to the other side, using each chapter as a stepping stone. So if your book is about helping someone overcome their fear of public speaking, when they get to the other side, they will have the knowledge, information, and blueprint to achieve that goal.

I hope you see the value in doing this critical research and reverse engineering your books. Don't make the mistake that the majority of authors make and "guess" or randomly pick a topic and title for their book.

Do the prework and you will reap amazing rewards.

I've abandoned many book ideas once I did the research and prework. The data I found just didn't support me investing my energy, time and money in writing that book on that topic. It's important to minimize your risk and increase your chances of long-term success.

Of course, you cannot predict how well any book will do, but taking the time to do this prework puts your book in a great position to do well.

In the next chapter, I'll be teaching you how to launch your book to the #1 bestsellers list and I'll also explain why this is so important to getting visibility on Amazon. In fact, without a book launch, your book will essentially be invisible on Amazon because the platform is highly competitive.

CHAPTER 7: NOTHING HAPPENS UNTIL YOU LAUNCH

"Without promotion, something terrible happens...Nothing!"
~ P.T. Barnum

A book launch is a designated time period (usually 1-5 days) in which you put all of your book marketing efforts to encourage readers to buy (or download) your book.

The goal of a book launch is to get the highest number of sales/downloads in the shortest amount of time so your book will hit as many Amazon Bestseller lists as possible.

We will talk more about how to consistently stay on a bestseller list, but the first goal is to reach the bestsellers list.

WHAT YOU SHOULD KNOW ABOUT AMAZON BESTSELLERS LISTS

Having your book on a Bestseller list = Visibility!

Having visibility on Amazon and being on bestsellers lists is like getting your website to Page 1 of Google. It's not easy to do, but when you do it, you will have a lot of eyeballs on your book!

Why is it important to be on the Bestsellers lists?

Because these bestseller lists are the most searched lists on Amazon, and when potential readers are searching for keywords on Amazon, you want your book to show up in the search results.

NOTE: Amazon does not always put books in the best categories when published (I'll talk about this more later). You must research the bestseller lists and categories, then submit a customer support ticket to have your book added to more categories.

How many bestseller lists are there?

It's estimated there are over 10,000 bestseller lists on Amazon. Think of broad categories like: Nonfiction, Fiction, Business, Memoirs, or Biographies. For every broad category there are dozens of sub-categories underneath them. The goal is for your book to show up on as many bestseller lists as possible so your book is reaching more people.

How to do you get your book on these bestsellers lists?

You book must have a high number of sales/downloads in a short period of time to get on bestsellers lists.

Then, to stay on the bestsellers list after the launch, you need consistent sales. We will talk about more about this shortly.

It's important to know that there are the PAID bestseller lists and FREE bestseller lists. For my clients, I typically start with a 2-day FREE launch and then get their books to the paid bestsellers list; this is a 2-stage or 2-step launch.

Why give away my book during a free book launch?

Unless you have a large email list or social media following, you will get a lot more exposure for your book doing a FREE bestseller launch. The difference could be possibly thousands of downloads on a FREE promotion vs. 100-300+ downloads on a PAID promotion (book launch). Also, if you include a link for a free gift in your book, you may influence readers to join your email list.

What happens when my book is on a bestsellers list?

- You have visibility now! Potential readers can find your book.
- "Bestseller lists" are the highly searched because when people want to solve a problem, they go looking for books in those categories and bestseller lists which is good for you.
- You book has been indexed by Amazon and is removed from obscurity.
- The mysterious Amazon Algorithm is triggered and if you get enough downloads and sales, Amazon will start marketing your book! Wouldn't it be nice to have Amazon promoting your book on various lists, to their Prime members, and even take out Pay-Per-Click ads and Facebook ads for your book? That is what happens for many authors when they get on the bestsellers list.

What is the Amazon Algorithm?

There is a lot of talk about the Amazon algorithm, but no one really knows exactly what it is. Just like no one can tell you what the Google algorithm is for being on Page 1 of the search results for your keywords.

However, I can tell you that based on my extensive testing and having done over 250 book launches, I've determined that the following criteria influences the Amazon Algorithm:

- Number of reviews (the more the better)
- Properly selected keywords
- Properly selected categories
- A book description containing keywords
- A title or subtitle with keywords, if possible
- Being on multiple bestsellers lists
- Being listed as a Hot New Release (to get on this list, you must do the book launch within 30 days of publishing your book)

Once you are #1 in your categories and your book is being downloaded and doing well, Amazon starts promoting your book in several different ways with its own internal marketing system.

I cannot guarantee that any book will stay a bestseller or do well forever (the market decides what it likes), however, I have many clients whose books have remained on these bestseller lists for months and years. Just be aware that you need to continue to market and promote your book after the book launch.

In addition to being on a bestsellers list, Amazon will often promote your book on other popular lists, such as:

- New for You
- Recommendations
- Based on your Browsing History
- Frequently Bought Together
- Hot New Releases (you can only get on this list within 30 days of publishing your book).
- Customers who bought this item also bought...
- Movers and Shakers
- Top Rated
- What Other Items Do Customers Buy After Viewing this Item?
- AND MORE!

When your book becomes a #1 BESTSELLER...you will hold that title for life!

You can add that title to your website, social media pages, your book cover, and use this esteemed title to elevate your credibility, authority, impact, and income.

SOME THINGS YOU MIGHT NOT KNOW:

- Amazon updates their bestsellers lists several times a day.

- There can be anywhere from 1-100 books on a bestsellers list.

- There are over 10,000 categories on Amazon; 99.9% of authors choose the wrong categories when publishing their book which means that their book is hidden from people who are looking for those types of books.

- Amazon allows you to choose only two broad categories when self-publishing on Amazon KDP. If you want your book to be a bestseller, you will have to do more research to find additional subcategories; then send a request to KDP to have your books added to those categories.

- You can become a bestseller on the FREE bestsellers list initially. However, ultimately, you want to be on the PAID bestsellers list.

- If you make your book exclusive to Amazon for 90 days through their "Kindle Select" program, you can use their promotional tools and offer your book for free for up to five days, every 90 days.

- It's important that before the book launch is scheduled you have the highest quality book cover as well as a magnetic book description that converts into sales!

I have an entire program and system for my launches, but I wanted to give you an overview of what to do when launching your books.

PRIOR TO THE LAUNCH:

- Make sure your book has five reviews before you hire book promoters. Note, I initially price the eBook at .99 so I can easily get sales and reviews.

- Have a compelling book description that piques the reader's interest coupled with a strong call to action that will make readers want to purchase your book.

- Select the best keywords for your book by doing keyword research using Publisher Rocket.

- Email KDP customer support to add your book to up to a total of 10 categories; this way your book can hit as many bestseller lists as possible. You want categories that are less competitive so your book can hit the top of the bestsellers lists.

PREPARING FOR THE LAUNCH:

- Schedule your book launch 14 days in advance ideally.

- Hire 5-10 promoters to promote your book during your designated launch. I do 2-day launches for my clients to the FREE bestsellers lists and 1-day launches for my own books to the PAID bestsellers lists at .99. *Note*: Some promoters only accept promotions for *free books*, and some only accept *paid promotions*. The promoters I use for free and paid launches are listed in the Resources section of this book.

- Set up social media posts with a service like Hootsuite so you are promoting your book to all of your social media sites on book launch day(s).

- If you have an email list, send out an email to your list(s) on book launch day(s).

WHAT TO DO ON BOOK LAUNCH DAY:

- Amazon updates these bestsellers lists at least a few times a day. I recommend checking your book's rankings later in the day on book launch day to give Amazon time to update them.

- Amazon will ONLY show the top 3 bestseller lists on your Amazon product/book page, however, your book will most likely be on an additional 10-20 bestsellers lists (if you selected the right categories). Amazon will show the subcategories you chose, but make sure you check the main categories as well. For example, if you selected the category of Small Business Franchise, it would show up as *Kindle eBooks>business & money>entrepreneurship & Small Business>franchises*. On your product page, Amazon will simply show your book as #1 in the *Franchises* category.

- Click on the bestseller list links to get screenshots of your book. If you don't see your book listed, make sure you are viewing the right list (paid vs. free).

- Create a marketing collage using a free service like PicMonkey or Canva and share your bestseller results on social media. You can check out collages I've created for my clients at: https://bestsellingauthorprogram.com/graduates/

WHAT TO DO AFTER THE LAUNCH

- Continue to market your book once you are a #1 Amazon Bestselling Author; launching and marketing a book is not a one-and-done event.

- Immediately set up Amazon Ads after the book launch with at least 500–1,000 keywords. This is critical to the success of your book after the launch.

- Add the bestseller logo to your covers and resubmit to Amazon (it can take 12-48 hours for approval).

- Immediately set up media interviews (podcasts and radio shows) once you become a bestselling author.

- If you did the 2-day free launch, and your book is not at the top of the paid bestsellers list within a week or so, then do a paid promotion to bump your book up even higher on the bestsellers lists.

- BookBub is great book promotion service for authors. You should apply for a *Featured Deal* to get in front of millions of book readers. Just know that you must wait 90 days after doing a book launch before you can submit your book to them.

- If you don't get accepted for a *Featured Deal* on BookBub, you can run BookBub ads, which are different and don't require the in-depth editorial review that a *Featured Deal* requires.

- If you don't get accepted by BookBub.com, then try Ereadernewstoday.com or RobinReads.com.

- I recommend hiring book promoters every 60-90 days to maintain your position on these bestsellers lists.
- Put 3D mock-ups of your book cover and links to your bestselling book on the home page of your website (if you have one.)
- Add something about your book to your autoresponder series so you are continually marketing your book to your list.

I teach this system to my students, and use it for my own book launches so it is a proven system.

I recently did a paid book launch for one of my books priced at .99. I hit over a dozen bestsellers lists, and reached #1 in four of those bestseller lists! I had over 40 sales coming off the $.99 2-day launch. I increased the price to $2.99 as soon as the 2-day launch was over. Because I have so many books, I feel that I can still stay on the top of the paid bestsellers lists with books priced at $2.99. If you notice your book rankings dropping suddenly, leave it at $.99 until it stabilizes on the paid bestsellers list and your Amazon Ads gain traction.

Once my books are selling consistently, I usually increase the eBook price to $3.99. You can test different price points for your books and increase them whenever you like.

What about print books you ask?

I only talk about kindle eBook pricing here because a launch isn't about your print book. I usually price my print books at $14.97, and Amazon pays me 60% of royalties after the cost of printing (this is what's known as print-on-demand), so I typically end up with a little over $6 for each print book sold. If someone buys my print book from a third party like Barnes and Noble, which goes through Amazon's backend (expanded distribution), the royalties are even lower – 40% minus the cost of printing.

When you are doing a FREE or PAID eBook launch, you will most likely sell some print books. I always publish the kindle and paperback at the same time.

It's very important that you do a proper book launch. Don't make the mistake many authors do by thinking readers will magically find your book after you hit the "publish" button. I can tell you, with 100% certainty, that until I do the launch, I don't see the increase of my monthly sales for my book because it is basically invisible on Amazon without a bestseller launch.

DO NOT SKIP THIS STEP!

CHAPTER 8: THE BOOK-A-MONTH (BAM) FRAMEWORK

If you started writing a book a month right now, how would that change your life?

I was recently watching a show on HGTV about a couple and their two young children who were relocating from Australia to Scotland so they could be close to the wife's family.

Since they both left their jobs in Australia and didn't have any income, they had a very limited budget of $1,000 a month to rent a home. The wife's dream was to live in a place with the "historic charm of Scotland." Unfortunately, the real estate agent couldn't find what she wanted within her budget. For only $200 more per month, she could have been living in her dream home.

They moved into a house she really didn't like, and she seemed highly disappointed. That made me realize how important an extra $200 a month income can be.

If you wrote a book a month, that could add up to thousands in income after several months.

It's hard to predict exactly how well a book will do. There are many niches, and every book is unique.

If you're ready to write a book a month and start earning passive income, let's start with planning out your year.

I always begin with an annual book schedule, which I recommend you create when you start this system, so you have a plan going into this.

Also, I believe you will sell more books if you stick to the same genre of books. Or you can do like I did and have two or three different genres and write three books for each series.

Below is my Book-A-Month Annual Publishing Chart template, which is available to download in my Facebook group.

Book-A-Month (BAM) Annual Publishing Chart

Title/ Subtitle	Genre/ Series	Outline/ Write	Edited	Cover Design	Proofed	Formatted	Book Description	ISBN	Pub. Date	Launch Date

I filled this out at the beginning of 2020:

Book-A-Month (BAM) Annual Publishing Chart

Title/Subtitle	Genre/Series	Outline/Write	Edited	Cover Design	Proofed	Formatted	Book Description	ISBN	Pub. Date	Launch Date
Quit Your Job & Follow Your Dreams	Biz/Career								Nov. 2019	Jan. 2020
How to Find Your Passion	Biz/Career								Jan. 2020	Feb. 2020
Work From Home & Make 6 Figures	Biz/Career								Feb. 2020	March 2020
Stop Living Paycheck-to-Paycheck	Biz/Money								March 2020	April 2020
Love Yourself Big	Self-Help/Women								April 2020	May 2020
28 Books to $100K	Biz/Author								May 2020	June 2020
Career Path Rehab	Biz/Career								June 2020	July 2020
Make Money While You Sleep	Biz/Money								July 2020	August 2020
Spandex Habits	Biz/Success								August 2020	Sept. 2020
Digital Retirement	Biz/Money								Sept. 2020	Oct. 2020
Red Dress Energy	Self-Help/Women								Oct. 2020	Nov. 2020
Secrets of Six Figure Women	Biz/Women								Nov. 2020	Dec. 2020

Now, this chart and publishing plan for the year isn't set in stone. Sometimes, I start to write a book and don't have the *energy* for the topic, so I shift gears.

With this annual publishing chart, at least I have a "flexible" plan to keep everything moving along because momentum is the name of the game.

When you write and publish books, you never know how much money you will make from each book. The $200 a month per book that I've mentioned throughout this book is just an estimate.

If we divide the number of books I've published by the number of months I've been doing this – my average earnings per book currently is $255 ($2300 per month divided by 9 months).

Let's take a look at the breakdown of the $2,300 a month I am currently making on my books:

- *How to Find Your Passion* – $1060
- *28 Books to $100K* – $552
- *Make Money While You Sleep* – $257
- *Work From Home & Make Six Figures* – $165
- *Stop Living Paycheck-to-Paycheck* – $99
- *Quit Your Job and Follow Your Dreams* – $67
- *Career Path Resuscitation* – $37 (Amazon originally blocked ads and I just got this resolved)
- *Bestseller in 30 Days* (old book) – $19
- *Backwards Book Launch* (old book) – $26
- *Love Yourself Big* – $9 (not yet launched)
- *Spandex Habits* – $6 (not yet launched)

It's really interesting when I look at the breakdown of income for my books. Currently, "How to Find Your Passion" accounts for 46% of my income; "28 Books to $100K", 24%; and "Make Money While Your Sleep," 11%. The remaining books make up the other 19%.

And that other 19% makes a big difference because it's $437 each month. Every little bit helps!

Of course, we don't have a crystal ball that tells us which books will take off. We can do all the keyword research, reverse engineering, and market research we want, but at the end of the day, the market decides what it likes.

When I wrote these books, I had no idea which ones would be the biggest sellers. The point is – you will sell more copies of some books than others, and that's okay; if you can generate an average of $200 to $300 per month on all your books combined, then you will be able to replace your Social Security income in approximately one year.

In the list of books above, two of them have not yet launched. Also, Amazon blocked the ads to one of my books, so I had to resolve that issue. The earnings are currently low for those titles, but should increase in the next few months.

Amazon has a lot of rules when running ads on their site, and if you violate those rules, they will not allow you to run ads.

Without ads, your books won't have much visibility. I highly recommend you run ads on all your books. I may end up writing an entire book about Amazon ads because it's that important.

My assistant, Alex Strathdee, runs all of my ads. You can reach out to him at:

https://www.advancedamazonads.com/

When you first publish a book, you won't make much money. That's why I included a chapter titled: "Nothing Happens Till You Launch." You must do a bestseller book launch so your book is on the most searched lists on Amazon – the bestseller lists. They truly are magical!

The Book-A-Month (BAM) Framework

- Do your Prework and Market Research before writing a word of your book
- Decide on which titles you will write for the year (complete the Annual Publishing Chart)
- Establish your writing schedule; you should have the manuscript for each month completed in 15 days.
- Use the remaining 15 days each month to work on editing, formatting, book cover design, writing a book description, and category and keyword research.
- Publish the completed book for that month.
- You will launch each book the following month after it is published.

Note: It would be next to impossible to write, edit, format, publish, and *launch* a high-quality book in 30 days. Especially since you need to get five reviews for your book in order to hire promoters to do the launch.

Sample Book-a-Month Schedule

Days 1-15

1. Write and organize the book.
2. Wait a few days, then review.
3. When you think of anything to add to or remove from your manuscript, make notes on your project folder to send to your editor/formatter.

Days 16-23

4. Send the manuscript to editor for initial edits.

5. Receive the first round of edits; review and accept or reject the changes.

6. Send the manuscript back to the editor for one more round of edits and/or final formatting.

7. Read the newly formatted and edited book word-for-word to catch anything that may have been missed in the initial round of edits.

8. While you are working on the manuscript, have the cover designer working on your cover.

Days 17-30

9. Write the book description, research the keywords and categories, and publish the book.

10. Do a soft launch to get 5-10 reviews.

Following Month

11. Launch the book

12. Start writing the next book.

The first time you do this, you'll learn a lot and you may feel overwhelmed, but it will get easier every month, I promise.

OUT-OF-POCKET EXPENSES TO PUBLISH A BOOK

"One of my books took more than a year to write, ten hours a day. Another took three weeks.
Both sell for the same price.
The quicker one outsold the other 20 to 1.
A $200 bottle of wine costs almost exactly as much to make as a $35 bottle of wine.
The cost of something is largely irrelevant, people are paying attention to its value.
Your customers don't care what it took for you to make something. They care about what it does for them."
~Seth Godin, Multiple Bestselling Author

Yes, there is a front-end financial and time investment, but if your books do well, you will make this money back.

- Editing - .03 cents per word on the low-end; so a 20,000 word manuscript would cost $600
- Formatting - $150-$250
- Cover Design - $100-$200
- Promoters - $125-$250

If finances are tight, you can find a cover designer on fiverr.com and pay $25-$50 for a decent cover. If you have tech skills, you can format the book yourself. I would never skimp on editing; always have your book professionally edited.

You can also hire promoters for as little as $60 or $75 and still get good results for a FREE promotion. PAID promotions are a little harder because readers are paying for the book, so you need to hire as many promoters as you possibly can. Even if you hire promoters, you also want to promote the book on your social media and to your email list.

HOW LONG SHOULD MY BOOKS BE?

I recommend that you write "short" books around 100 pages long.

In the past, big publishing houses could charge more for longer books. There was also a high-demand from consumers who wanted to read longer books.

However, people now have less time than ever and decreased attention spans.

Readers want short books!

Top 10 Reasons To Write Short Reads Books

1. Time and attention are in short supply, so there is a greater demand from readers for quick reads.
2. It's easier to write a short book focused on one topic than a longer book with multiple topics.
3. It takes less time to write fewer words (I wrote the bulk of this book in a week).
4. Volume boosts your visibility (especially on Amazon). Writing multiple high-quality books can attract repeat readers who will follow you.

5. Short books involve less risk. Because you are not investing a considerable amount of time or money in creating these books, less than expected sales will not greatly impact you. In fact, you will learn what works and what doesn't work and use that knowledge when writing more books.
6. You can create a series of short books that explore your favorite subjects in greater depth than you could do in one chapter of a single, larger book.
7. Much of the data shows that people do not finish reading long books. Since shorter books require less time to read, there is a greater chance people will actually read your entire book.
8. Amazon has a specific category for short books called "Short Reads." You can't select this category when publishing on KDP, but if the number of pages in your book matches the criteria in that Short Reads category, Amazon will include your book in that category, giving it more exposure.
9. You can set a lower price your eBook and get a higher quantity of sales.
10. You can niche and grow rich by writing short books in very narrow categories and do extremely well.

SHORT BOOKS VS. LONG BOOKS

I spent a year writing the second edition of my book, "Quit Your Job and Follow Your Dreams," which ended up being 250 pages!

When I decided to do this "book a month" experiment, I wrote "How to Find Your Passion: 23 Questions that Can Change Your Entire Life" in about three weeks. I published it within 30 days, and right now, this is my bestselling book. It outsells "Quit Your Job and Follow Your Dreams" 10 to 1. I believe it's because people want shorter books that contain action items they can use to get quick results.

We live in a high-tech, fast-paced world. Most of us are extremely distracted and our time is fragmented. We face constant interruptions from emails, texts, phone calls, Facebook, Twitter, Instagram, and more. Gone are the days when people will buy a manifesto and block out their entire weekend to leisurely read.

Consequently, attention spans have diminished. The desire to learn new things still exists but most people want to learn faster.

Consider this when writing books. Instead of writing a book on the A-Z of Marketing, write a series of short books that each focus on one narrow topic. For example, the series could include books on these topics: Writing Persuasive Sales Copy; Creating Facebook Ads; Building a Profitable Blog; How to Create a Webinar, etc.

Think micro-topics instead of macro-topics.

6 TYPES OF EASY-TO-WRITE SHORT BOOKS

1. List or tip book
2. Step-by-step guide
3. Q&A interview focused on a specific topic

4. Single-question deep dive
5. Collection book (for example, top strategies, top recipes, or top performers in an industry)
6. Extended blog post – if you have a popular blog post, expand on it and publish it as a short book

Return on Investment (ROI)

I've written long books as well as short books, and shorter books provide a much higher return on investment.

Writing shorter books saves you time while increasing your revenue. Let's say you spend one full year writing one book (like I have and many of my clients have done), and you earn $200 a month from that one book. If you were writing a book a month, you could have written 12 books, each earning $200 a month, and your income would be $2,400 per month instead of $200 per month!

Additionally, you are more likely to finish writing and publishing a shorter book because writing 50,000 to 100,000 words can be a daunting task.

I work with clients who have spent years working on their "one book."

I encourage you to write short books. You can write the book in about two weeks, and then finish everything else in the next two weeks.

When I send my final manuscript to my editor (I recommend always using a professional editor), she reviews it and sends it back to me with changes marked in the document. I review her suggested changes and accept or reject them. Then, I wait a day or two and read the book again word-for-word (which is easy to do with a short book), and I always find a few typos and some changes I want to make.

A 250+ page book would require too much time to write, edit, and review, and I would not be able to publish a book a month with that many pages.

So, keep it short and save yourself the overwhelm! Readers want short books!

WRITING SHORT BOOKS IS A LOT LIKE BLOGGING

For years, I wrote long copy blogs every month. I think that prepared me for writing a book a month.

If you're a blogger, you have an advantage because you can potentially expand on some of your blog posts to create short books. Additionally, you have been writing consistent content; writing a book a month is like writing 5-10 blog posts. That's a good way to break it down.

Now that you have the book-a-month (BAM) framework, next we're going to talk about your Social Security Retirement Blueprint.

CHAPTER 9: SOCIAL SECURITY REPLACEMENT BLUEPRINT

Imagine a world where you get to spend your time on things that fulfill you like painting, biking, crafting, traveling, reading, hiking, baking, bowling, pottery, dancing, sewing, genealogy, weight training, jewelry making, yoga, karate, camping, canoeing, archery, rafting, rock climbing, snowboarding, golf, flying, gardening, sailing, surfing, swimming, tennis, wine making or wine drinking.

Sounds amazing, right?

You can potentially retire in 12-24 months and have time and financial freedom if you follow my book a month system.

THE EXPERTS ARE WRONG

The experts now say millennials need $2 million saved to retire by age 65. Really? How many people do you know who retired with $2 million in the bank? This goal is highly unlikely and unrealistic.

CNBC reported that one in three American have less than $5,000 saved for retirement, and that Baby Boomers (like me) have a median savings of $24,280. That means a Baby Boomer that has $4,000 in living expenses who retires can live on their savings for only six short months.

With all the changes going on in the world, people are tired of the "work 30-40 years for a company and retire old."

Many millennials have figured out how to retire in their 20's and skip the decades of job prison.

My assistant, Alex Strathdee, is an excellent example of this new millennial mindset. Alex graduated from Virginia Tech with a degree in programming and coding. Straight from university, he landed a 6-figure job with a large IT company. He was one of my clients in my bestselling author program and shortly after we launched his book, he inquired about coming to work for me. Alex was 23 years old at the time.

I was surprised he wanted to work for me, since I assumed he was living the dream. He went on to explain that he could not see himself sitting in a cubicle writing code for the next 30 or 40 years! He decided he was going to do freelance work and travel the world.

So, I hired him, and within one year, Alex has created six figures in income doing Amazon ads for me and my clients while traveling the world.

Alex used his coding skills to write software to set up thousands of keywords and campaigns while creating Amazon ads for authors to generate sales for their books.

A large part of the success I've had with my books is because of Alex's genius when it comes to Amazon ads!

LOSE THE TRADING HOURS FOR DOLLARS MINDSET AND CREATE PASSIVE INCOME

As I said in the introduction, after I wiped out my 401K and lost the million-dollar house to a short sale, I had to start over. I did not want to play the stock market game, invest in real estate, or learn how to be a day trader.

I wanted to use skills I already had to create income that would pay all of my bills. My estimate is that I should hit that magic number ($4,000 per month) by mid-2021.

Remember, I started this process in January 2020 and I could potentially stop working and retire early in just 12-18 months!

Another benefit of creating passive income to cover your bills if you are a business owner, is that it allows you to be more selective with the clients with whom you choose to work.

Even if you're not trying to retire early, how would you like to make an extra $1000, $2000, $4000 or $5000 per month? How would that make a difference in your life?

Let's be honest – passive income isn't totally passive is it?

You have to put in a lot of sweat equity in the beginning, before you reap the rewards down the road. But wouldn't you rather put in 12-24 months and work your a$$ off for two years than trudge along for the next 30-40 years in a job you hate making somebody else rich?

WHERE DID SOCIAL SECURITY COME FROM?

Let's look at how Social Security was created...

Franklin D. Roosevelt (FDR) signed the Social Security Act of 1935 to provide aid and benefits for families during the Great Depression. The problem was the government didn't have any way to fund this new program as it would take enormous amounts of money to begin giving cash to every retired and disabled person in the U.S.

So what's a President to do?

The government's solution was to set up a system in which the younger generations fund the older generations retirement benefits. Consequently, FDR implemented the Social Security tax on current working Americans. That tax revenue is used to make payments to currently retired Americans.

So that 6.2% Social Security tax that is deducted from your paycheck is not in a special account with your name on it; it is being used to make payments to those currently receiving Social Security benefits.

When Social Security first started, the number of people working vastly outnumbered the number of retired Americans. In other words, for each retired person collecting Social Security, multiple people were working and paying into the fund providing payments.

In 1940, when the first benefits were paid out, there were 159.4 workers per covered beneficiary. Setting up the tax this way seemed like there would be more than enough money for future retired Americans.

Except it wasn't.

Baby Boomers (those born between 1946 and 1964) quickly became the largest generation in the US, and the trust fund ballooned as they reached working age.

What the government, however, failed to account for was that this Baby Boomer population would also eventually retire; that impact would be devastating because there would be fewer Americans working per retired Americans.

By 2013, there were only 2.8 workers per covered beneficiary.

Another negative consideration is that with the decline in the number of children per family, the size of the workforce will be smaller.

In response to these compounding problems, the government has pushed back the retirement age, increased the tax, and lowered benefits over time – but not rapidly or significantly enough.

As it stands at the time of this writing, the funds will be fully depleted by 2035.

What was once considered a robust and strong program, now has massive problems.

The point I'm trying to make is: I wouldn't solely count on Social Security to fund your retirement.

WHAT ABOUT PENSIONS?

Pensions were a defined benefit plan offered by employers or the government; in exchange for a long and loyal tenure at a company, the company pays you a portion of your salary until your death. Unfortunately, pensions are becoming extinct because they are too costly for employers to maintain. That's where 401K's came in…

THE 411 ON 401K'S

These are employee-contributed plans. The money is typically invested in the stock market by a third party, and you may or may not have the money when you retire. What goes up, also comes down.

Years ago, when my kids were little, the house I was renting was being put up for sale and I had to move quickly. I didn't have the money to purchase a home, so my very generous brother helped his sister out. He pulled $60,000 out of the stock market and put the down payment on a beautiful house for me and my three children.

Luckily, the housing market was on the upswing in 2000 and I was able to refinance and pay him back with interest within two years. I remember what he said to me when I paid him back, "I'm glad I loaned you that money. The stock market crashed right after I pulled it out and I would have lost it all."

I don't know about you, but I don't like investing in things I don't understand, that I can lose thousands of dollars instantly, and couldn't easily explain to a 12-year-old.

I got ripped off by a network marketing company because I didn't understand their smoke and mirrors compensation plan. Ask around, I'm sure you'll hear lots of horror stories about these companies.

I'm not saying there aren't a few good network marketing companies out there – Mary Kay has stood the test of time – but I would rather build my own business than someone else's.

Social Security Replacement Blueprint to Create Your Retirement income

Estimated Social Security Income	Estimated Monthly Book Income	Number of Books Needed to Hit Target Income ($200/mo. income average from each book)
$1,600	$1,600	8 books
$1800	$1800	9 books
$2000	$2000	10 books
$2200	$2200	11 books
$2400	$2400	12 books
$2600	$2600	13 books
$2800	$2800	14 books
$3000	$3000	15 books

Time will pass whether you write a book a month or not. So why not secure your financial future by writing a book a month? It's a powerful wealth-building tool, especially if you are unprepared for retirement like I was.

I have so much less stress and more confidence in my future knowing that I can retire in 2021 with the means to pay all of my living expenses if I desire to.

The sky is the limit.

You don't have to write a book a month; you could write a book every two months; or one every quarter. But I like the momentum I have from writing a book a month.

CASE STUDY OF AN AUTHOR MAKING $25,000 PER MONTH

I want to inspire and motivate you with real stories. Earlier I mentioned Steven Higgins, a fiction writer, who is now making $40,000 per month from writing a book a month.

Another fellow author, Marc Reklau, who is the author of over a dozen bestselling books, is making over $25,000 per month now from his books!

I remember when Marc was making just $1000 a month on his books and really struggling. He persisted and was determined to make a living as a full-time writer.

Marc is now living his dream because he didn't give up! I love seeing his pictures on social media in different countries, on his house boat in Spain, and enjoying life.

I know that Marc has invested thousands of dollars in his education and on Amazon ads; because of his time and money investment, he has been successful.

You can check our all of Marc's books here: https://www.amazon.com/Marc-Reklau/e/B00IZALH04/

Think about the freedom and options you will have when you can generate your monthly income.

This path is not for everyone, but if you have a message to share with the world and you want to build a *Digital Retirement*, it won't take too long to exceed your Social Security income.

YOU HAVE THE POWER TO CREATE YOUR OWN DESTINY.

CHAPTER 10: CLOSING THOUGHTS

Years ago, I was working for an attorney who had a private practice. I was the paralegal, legal secretary, and his right-hand assistant. I was young and naively thought I was irreplaceable.

I worked hard, and felt that entitled me to time off and long breaks.

One day when my boss was out of town, I decided to go run an errand that should have taken an hour and a half, but took three hours because of traffic and other delays.

When I returned to the office, I found out he had been calling the secretary every thirty minutes looking for me, and I was fired on the spot.

That taught me a valuable lesson – we are all replaceable.

I was a single mother at the time, living paycheck-to-paycheck and didn't have any money in savings.

I never want to be in that position again, which is probably why I'm so fanatical about creating multiple streams of income. You never know when one stream will run dry.

For years, my only source of income was from my day job in the legal field. Now, I have at least 4-6 income streams at any given time. I like to work smart, not hard.

I wrote this book to inspire my readers to think outside the box and not depend on one income stream for your retirement, or for that matter, your livelihood.

Maybe those predictions are wrong and Social Security will be here after 2035, but it's better to be over-prepared than under-prepared, right?

I know we can't predict everything that will happen in the future, but when you have the ability to create your own income, you have more options for your future.

In March 2020, a worldwide pandemic hit and things changed drastically for a lot of people; many industries were disrupted, and millions of people lost their jobs and their ability to earn a living.

Change is inevitable and whether we like it or not, sometimes change is thrust upon us.

The publishing business actually became busier for me because *more* people had *more* time to write books.

It's easy to discount the future by saying, "I have to focus on the present," but the future will become the present one day, and we must ask ourselves now, "Am I prepared for my future?"

Writing a book a month is just one path that can help you prepare for your retirement, your future, and even provide a new income stream for you.

I think to some extent we've all been sleepwalking when it comes to our finances and our future. Sometimes it takes a major wake-up call like a pandemic to cause us to reflect on how we've been living our lives and how we might want to do things differently in our future.

I hope this book has inspired you to think about your future differently, and how to realize you have the power to change it.

Wishing you much success!

Michelle Kulp

RESOURCES

It can take years to find great book promoters, cover designers, formatters, and editors. I currently use the following resources for my books, or these have been recommended to me by other authors.

PROMOTERS: PAID VS. FREE

It's important to understand that there are promoters who will only promote your book when it is free (which you can do by signing up for Amazon's Kindle Select program inside your KDP account) and there are other promoters who only do paid (which typically means your book price is reduced to .99 cents). Last, there are some promoters that do free and paid launches. I just wanted to point this out.

Promoters for FREE Book Launches

- RobinReads.com/genre-divide/
- BookTweeters.com/ - home –
- eReaderIQ.com/authors/submissions/dds/
- Fiverr.com/bknights
- JamesHMayfield.com/book-promotions/ *only does free
- FreeBooksy.com/freebooksy-feature-pricing/m

Promoters for Books Priced at Least $0.99

***Instead of freebooksy, hire bargainbooksy:

- BargainBooksy.com/sell-more-books-2/

- BookSends.com/advertise.php
- eReaderNewsToday.com/bargain-and-free-book-submissions/ - toggle-id-1 – *****must be submitted 10-14 days in advance!

*90 days after you do a #1 book launch, you can apply for a BookBub featured deal:

- BookBub Featured Deal, Price Varies: BookBub.com/partners/pricing

**If you don't get accepted, try running ads on their platform:

- BookBub Ads Anytime, Price Varies: Insights.BookBub.com/introducing-bookbub-ads-promote-any-book-any-time/

BOOK COVER DESIGNERS

- 99designs.com/ebook-cover-design
- 100covers.com
- FosterCovers.com
- GraceMyCanvas.com
- Archangelink.com/book-covers/
- FionaJaydeMedia.com/non-fiction/
- Fiverr.com/designa2z
- Fiverr.com/cal5086
- Fiverr.com/galuhh
- Fiverr.com/lauria

- Fiverr.com/vikiana
- Fiverr.com/germancreative
- My designer is Zeljka: vukojeviczeljka@gmail.com

FORMATTERS

- **Heather Mize at My Book Team** – heather@MyBookTeam.com

TEMPLATES:

For DIY formatting, you can get some great templates at BookDesignTemplates.com

EDITORS (All editors I have used)

- **Heather Mize** – heather@MyBookTeam.com
- **Lori Duff, Esq** – lori@loriduffwrites.com
- **Pamela Gossiaux** – pam@pamelagossiaux.com
- **Hollace Donner** – Pailmoritz@yahoo.com

GHOSTWRITERS

- **Lori Duff, Esq.** – LoriDuffWrites.com/lori-writes-for-you-expert-ghost-writer/ghost-writing-rates
- **Emily Crookston, Ph.D.** – ThePocketPHD.com

COPYWRITERS

- Rob Schultz – ProfitSeduction.com
- BestPageForward.net/blurbs

AMAZON ADS

- **Alex Strathdee** – AdvancedAmazonAds.com

ONLINE COURSE PLATFORM

I use Thinkific for my "Client Learning Portal," which is essentially my online course/program/training: http://try.thinkific.com/michellekulp6975

PUBLIC RELATIONS

- **Christina Daves** – www.ChristinaDaves.com

SOFTWARE I USE

***Aweber:** http://michellekulp.aweber.com

***Bluehost:** http://www.bluehost.com/track/mkulp

***Pop-Up domination:** https://app.popupdomination.com/aff/5d4a184df5895d7c596f5242

***Publisher Rocket**
https://mkulp--rocket.thrivecart.com/publisher-rocket/

KDSpy
https://mkulp--leadsclick.thrivecart.com/kdspy-v5/

Bestseller Ranking Pro:
https://mkulp--tckpublishing.thrivecart.com/bestseller-ranking-pro-special-lifetime/

Book Report: https://app.getbookreport.com/

HTML Book Description Generator:
https://kindlepreneur.com/amazon-book-description-generator/

BOOK PRINTERS:

http://www.printopya.com/book

ILLUSTRATORS

www.Gemini-h.com/illustrations

www.Instagram.com/art_of_geminih

Note: Some of the links listed above are affiliate links, which means I may receive a commission at no cost to you if you purchase from those links.

Printed in Poland
by Amazon Fulfillment
Poland Sp. z o.o., Wrocław